coffee time

The Deutsche Nationalbibliothek lists this publication in the Deutsche Nationalbibliografie; detailed bibliographical data are available on the internet at http://dnb.dnb.de

ISBN 978-3-03768-105-3
© 2012 by Braun Publishing AG
www.braun-publishing.ch

2nd edition 2013

Selection of projects: Michelle Galindo, Manuela Roth,
Chris van Uffelen
Editorial staff: Antje Bertz, Jan Schneider
Text editing and translation: Judith Vonberg
Art direction: Michaela Prinz

michelle galindo

coffee

contemporary cafés

time

BRAUN

Content

Coffee Houses
by Markus Hattstein

What is it that defines a "coffee house"? It's a difficult question to answer and indeed one that can never be answered definitively; for every coffee house since the concept first emerged reflects the tastes and preferences of the particular era and society in which it exists. Each coffee house can therefore be read in some way as a representation of its time and the history of coffee houses as the story of changing, developing societies. Coffee houses have always been more than simply a place to drink coffee – they are places of social interaction where information can be exchanged, ideas disseminated and the latest fashions paraded.

The first coffee houses

The first coffee houses were reputedly established in Constantinople (now Istanbul) in 1554. Modest shacks or tents were erected with simple seating arrangements – benches running along the walls or mats on the floor. Copper pots filled with hot water were balanced on top of tiled stoves whose fires burned continually – a sight still common today in some Oriental countries. Guests looked on while ground coffee was poured into the pot and the beverage prepared. Coffee sellers could also be found out on the streets, walking through cities offering the hot beverage to interested passersby.

Coffee arrived in western Europe sometime after 1620 and began to revolutionize earlier drinking habits and tastes. Within just a few years three new drinks – coffee, tea and cocoa – had altered the drinking habits of Europeans forever. The first coffee tavern was reputedly established in Vienna in 1647, while coffee houses in Oxford and London followed soon after, in 1650 and 1652 respectively. The first Dutch coffee house opened in The Hague in 1673 and the first German varieties in Bremen (1673) and Hamburg (1677) weren't far behind. Dark and cramped beer taverns or shops, modified a little for their new purpose, often served as premises for these early enterprises. Known as "Caffee-Gewölbe" ("coffee vaults") or "Coffee-Stuben" ("coffee shops"), they were unornamented and furnished with plain wooden tables which were pushed together as necessary, and simple wooden benches, later replaced by wooden chairs. At first, visitors paid a fixed fee on entry (one penny in England), while later it became common practice for a cashier to give out tokens which were then cashed in for each cup of coffee.

Even in western Europe, the first coffee taverns were run by Oriental immigrants – Greeks, Armenians, Turks and Arabs, who faced fierce opposition from local guilds and fought a bitter and highly competitive battle against beer taverns and public houses. Vienna, later renowned for its coffee houses, was the site of one such battle. The rumor was spread by coffee house opponents that the imperial spy Georg Franz Kolschitzky had stolen some sacks of coffee beans (which the Viennese initially mistook for camel feed) from the defeated Turks as they fled from Vienna in 1683 and used them to open the first Viennese coffee shop. Yet it was actually an Armenian called Johannes Diodato who secured a monopoly in 1685 from Leopold I on the sale of coffee and tea in the city, a privilege that lasted 20 years. Later, it was mostly English and Dutch traders who ran the coffee houses in the towns and cities of Europe.

Until the 19th century only men were allowed to enter coffee houses (the female cashier being the sole exception), and indeed many cities and governments chose to enshrine this custom in law. Yet as coffee houses became increasingly well-established in European cities, so the dissatisfaction with the "gin palace" culture of these male-dominated institutions became increasingly vocal. This dissatisfaction manifested itself at first in newly erected coffee tents and pavilions as well as street taverns which could meet a growing demand from coffee drinkers to enjoy fresh air and a nice view along with their beverage.

left: scene in an English coffeehouse. A gentleman showered his opponent a hot cup of coffee in his face, after both had different opinions in a debate.

right: Jean Béraud, La Pâtisserie Gloppe, 1889. Oil on wood, 38 x 53 cm.

Eventually, Viennese lawmakers recognized this need and enshrined "Schanigärten" (pavement cafés) in law as fenced garden areas located in front of each café and belonging to the café owner.

Soon after, the first sumptuously decorated, light-filled coffee houses began to appear, spawning many others all over Europe in a similarly ostentatious style. The international standard was set with *Café Procope* (named after its founder, the Sicilian Procopio Cultelli), established in Paris in 1686, with its tables made from slabs of marble and walls entirely of mirrors generating an illusion of vastness (a feature still to be found in many modern coffee shops). The desire among the social elite of the period both to observe and to be observed had never been met quite so flamboyantly as in *Café Procope*, which inspired numerous similarly boastful coffee houses in the central squares and streets of towns such as Venice. In 1720, *Caffé Florian* opened its doors to coffee drinkers for the first time and, before long, no self-respecting tourist to the city could leave without paying a visit. From the beginning of the 19th century, every coffee house that took at least a little pride in itself decked out its rooms with mirrored cabinets and luxurious, dainty interiors, so that many establishments exuded the air of small Rococo castles. The legendary *Silberne Kaffeehaus* ("Silver Coffee House"), which was opened by Ignaz Neuner in Vienna in 1808, served coffee in silver pots, while some featured coffee fountains or other ingenious technical gimmicks. The desire among guests to read over their coffee led to the introduction of more light in most coffee houses – in earlier days, guests had to pay a supplementary charge for candles, while these were later provided as a matter of course. As gas and then electric light were invented, larger coffee houses everywhere became some of the first public institutions to make use of these innovations. It seems that a few coffee house owners even seemed to make it their mission to overwhelm their guests with every possible modern luxury and grandiose feature. Perhaps the most famous example is the golden clad *Café New York* in Budapest, opened in 1894, reminiscent of a baroque church with its twisted columns in the interior.

From about 1850, chairs made from curved wood began to dominate the interior of simpler coffee houses. Named "Thonet" chairs after the furniture manufacturer Michael Thonet, these have been a key element of classic coffee house design ever since. More luxurious coffee houses often featured stylish "bent wood" chairs.

After 1800, genuine coffee houses began to find themselves facing competition. On the one hand, restaurants began to spring up outside France (where the first of those establishments had appeared) and many of them now combined eating areas with a designated area for serving coffee or even with their own coffee house. On the other hand, hotels discovered their guests' growing taste for coffee and opened their own coffee rooms, at first with separate areas for men and women. Even today, the lounge of a hotel in England is called a "coffee room", a name that originates in the early days of hotels, when hotel rooms were dark and sparsely furnished and all the activities of the guests, as well as meals, took place in the communal coffee room.

The bourgeois coffee house

The crowd found inside coffee houses has not always been diverse. Since the nobility and the upper classes preferred to savor their Oriental beverages privately in their own parlors, and the lower classes were happier in beer taverns, the coffee house of the 18th century became an institution of the bourgeoisie, more accurately, of bourgeois intellectuals. During this period, the custom developed of stocking coffee houses with copies of the most important national and local newspapers, which guests could read free of charge – it's now impossible to imagine a coffee house culture without this custom.

Leading the way were England and the Netherlands with their strong democratic traditions, as well as pre-revolutionary, newly enlightened France. The middle classes of the 18th century were hungry for education and information, both of which could be found in the innumerable newspapers and journals being printed in this period – before long, coffee houses in towns and cities across Europe were offering themselves as places where this desire to read and become informed could be met. Numerous debating and progressive pedagogical societies, mostly of a patriotic and democratic tendency, established

regular meetings in coffee houses. In England, bookshop owners began to seek locations near coffee houses, café owners set up bookshops and publishers came to coffee houses to advertise upcoming publications. Coffee houses that were particularly known for their encouragement of pedagogy earned the name "Penny Universities". In France, virtually all of the key enlightenment thinkers along with their critics and followers were regular coffee house visitors.

However, it was not only education and news that the middle classes sought in these coffee house gatherings – they also wanted to be entertained. As a result, games of cards and chance as well as board games became regular features of coffee house life, and it was not long before every half-decent coffee house had its own billiard table. There were chess cafés and coffee houses with their own games rooms – named in Vienna after a card game, "Tarockzimmer" ("tarot rooms") – and separate smoking saloons.

A few enterprising coffee house owners even began to entertain their guests with performances by singers and orchestras – the Venetian *Caffé Florian* even had its very own orchestra and, before long, no coffee could be drunk in a Viennese coffee house without musical accompaniment from a string player, often influenced by "Schrammelmusik", a style of Viennese folk music named for the composers Johann and Josef Schrammel. In the 19th and early 20th centuries, waltzes by Strauss and other similarly undemanding styles of music found particular favor among the audiences of these new "concert cafés". Cabaret and variety performances also found their way into coffee houses at the end of the 19th century, while some establishments were transformed into picture palaces in the early 1900s for the new medium of film.

The emphasis on the bourgeois family in the Biedermeier era led to the dissolution of "men only" coffee houses in about 1870, replaced by family cafés that welcomed women. The public coffee culture was revolutionized: not only did cafés become the preferred destination for Sunday family outings, but "women only" cafés began to appear, often coupled with confectioners' shops. Exquisite cakes and sweet dainties were served alongside coffee, while the coffee itself was refined and enhanced with a range of added ingredients. Cafés became meeting points for the card games and coffee parties of slightly older ladies, mocked as "coffee aunts" or "coffee sisters". Cafés with specialty cakes became hugely popular, for example, *Café Sprüngli* in Zurich with its specialty chocolates, or *Café Prinzess* in Regensburg (opened in 1686), reputedly where individual filled chocolates (known in German as "Pralinen") were invented. The bourgeois café was no longer primarily a place for debates on politics and current affairs, but rather the epitome of comfort and relaxation. The presence of numerous cafés or coffee houses in every town and city in Europe, most prominently in the metropolises of the Habsburg Empire, was now taken for granted. In 1900, more than 600 coffee houses could be found in Vienna alone and more than 500 in Budapest.

The political coffee house and the working class café

In almost all European countries during the development of the coffee house, the instruments of state looked mostly unfavorably on them — a result of the free discussion and debate that was enjoyed there and the subsequent development of increasing numbers of informed citizens. In England — the leading coffee-drinking nation in Europe before its citizens turned their attention to tea — the coffee house had scarcely become established before it became a central location for political quarrels between various parties and societies. The liberal Whigs and the conservative Tories each had their own preferred coffee houses and, before long, the term "coffee house politician" became widespread as a description of the self-important, grumbling politician often found there. Returning from exile in 1660, the Stuart King Charles II soon recognized the coffee house as a breeding ground for dissent and banned coffee houses completely in 1675. He had not reckoned, however, with the resulting uproar from both coffee house owners and their patrons, and he was forced to repeal the ban later that same year. In about 1700, there were around 2,000 coffee houses in London, and in 1730, the author Henry Fielding created a box office hit with his play, "The Coffee-House Politician".

In pre-revolutionary France it was the parties who would later initiate the French Revolution whose followers met and developed their ideas in coffee houses; in 1789, Paris alone could boast 800 of them. It was in the Parisian *Café de Foy* that "Les Enragés" ("the Enraged Ones", a group of radicals active during the French Revolution) agreed on their demand for the universal arming of the people and eventually founded the Jacobin Party, who met in various coffee houses that then became known as "Jacobin Cafés". Many later popular speakers for the revolution, such as the journalist Camille Desmoulins, tested their ideas and rhetoric in front of coffee house audiences before braving the larger, more critical audiences out on the streets. In the late 1790s, leading politicians and party representatives continued to meet regularly in Parisian coffee houses.

German Jacobins, too, chose to gather in coffee houses, most notably in Mainz, and this habit became so closely associated with them that they were often described as "Kaffeehauspolitiker" (coffee-house politicians) in police reports.

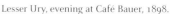
Lesser Ury, evening at Café Bauer, 1898.

The famed "emigrant cafés" should also be mentioned in the context of political coffee houses. Frequented mostly by politically persecuted intellectuals from Germany, Italy, Poland and Russia, most were located in France, although a few could be found in other liberal countries such as England and Switzerland. Georg Büchner, Ferdinand Freiligrath and Wilhelm Weitling could often be found at such cafés in Switzerland, and Heinrich Heine, Ludwig Börne, Karl Marx and Giuseppe Mazzini in French coffee houses. The "*German Coffee House*" in London became a meeting point for German immigrants who had been forced to flee after the suppression of the 1848 Revolution, and the *Café des Boulevards* welcomed a similar clientele in Brussels. In Geneva, socialist Russian immigrants gathered in *Café-Brasserie Landolt,* which played host to key figures including Lenin, who could often be found playing chess there.

The working classes needed a little more time before they found their place in coffee house culture – it was an institution that had long been reserved for the bourgeoisie and the intelligentsia of European society. Socialist politicians, however, began to use coffee houses as locations for educating the lower classes, both in politics and more generally – a method which also functioned as a means of reducing the otherwise excessive consumption of alcohol among the working classes in pubs and gin palaces. As a result, many coffee houses became known as "proletarian cafés" or "people's coffee houses", and village pubs began offering coffee alongside alcohol or even became coffee shops. In more urban areas, new coffee shops were built specifically for cab drivers and travelers, who drank their morning coffee in these "Kaffeeklappen" (as they became affectionately known among Berliners). Workers' organizations and working class parties met regularly in locked rooms in coffee houses, and even temperance societies began to voice their approval of both cafés and coffee for their promotion of a healthier way of life than one fuelled by alcohol. After 1876 vast "people's coffee halls" began to open in every large industrial city, supported by state and charitable health care institutions, for the mass provision of coffee and tea at little cost; in 1888 there were already 28 of them across Germany, at least one in every city.

From this period until well into the age of Metternich, coffee houses and their guests were often under state surveillance and were frequently featured in the reports of police informants and spies. In Berlin in the years preceding the 1848 German revolution, *Café Stehely* played a key role as a meeting place for the "Doctor's Club", a gathering of young Hegelians. Among this group were several figures who would later alter the course of German philosophy including Karl Marx and Friedrich Engels, both of whom were members for several years. The above-mentioned *Silberne Kaffeehaus* in Vienna became the meeting point for liberal opponents of the Metternichs in Austria, a cause supported by the café's owner Ignaz Neuner. The intellectual impetus for the European revolutions of 1830 and 1848/49 was nurtured to a great extent in metropolitan coffee houses – the Venetian regularly hosted the secret revolutionary societies known as the "Carbonari", while democratically minded Hungarians met under the leadership of the poet Sándor Petöfi in *Café Pilvax* in Budapest. Both movements then used these coffee houses as the locations from which to launch their assault on the Habsburg absolutism that they detested.

Congestion on one of the first espresso bars in London in the 1950s.

left: Vincent van Gogh, Café Terrace at Night, 1888.
Oil on canvas, 81 x 65,5 cm.
right: Juan Gris, Man in the Café, 1912.
Oil on canvas, 128.2 x 88 cm.

The literary coffee house

Scarcely any other image of coffee house culture has become so engrained in the popular imagination as that of a gathering place for artists, particularly literary figures. Ever since the first coffee house was built, painters have found inspiration within their walls – to name just a few, Auguste Renoir, Edgar Degas, Toulouse-Lautrec, Vincent van Gogh and Pablo Picasso have all produced masterpieces inspired by coffee houses. Picasso and Georges Braques developed Cubism in the Parisian *Café Aux Deux Magots*, while the *Café le Dôme* in the same city later became the preferred haunt of a range of famous painters. Several coffee house owners commissioned renowned sculptors to embellish the interiors of their cafés, while others paid artists to paint the walls and fixtures or turned their entire enterprises into works of art, of which the *Caffè Pedrocchi* in Padua is a fabulous example.

Above all, however, it was men of letters – authors, critics and journalists – who met regularly in coffee houses and read newspapers, indulged in people-watching, discussed current affairs, drank coffee, smoked and enjoyed heated debates. Satires, plays and novels, even poems, have been conceived and created in coffee houses, and there are a few works of literature (and their authors) that are almost inconceivable without the coffee house as a backdrop. Yet this relationship is a mutual one – not only has the coffee house made the creation of many works possible, so too have many works and their authors immortalized particular coffee houses.

This relationship has the longest tradition in Paris. In *Café Procope*, Voltaire and Diderot rubbed shoulders with a group of writers and actors whose ideas and judgments were absorbed eagerly by Europe's increasingly educated citizens. In the 19th century, the regular coffee house visitor Honoré de Balzac began to chronicle the coffee house lifestyle. In around 1890, Stéphane Mallarmé held court in the Parisian *Café Voltaire* as a sort of poet laureate, in a group that included Rimbaud, Verlaine and Gauguin. At the end of the 1930s, *Café de Flore*, open since 1865 and frequented by André Breton and the surrealists, became the center of French intellectual life. Jean-Paul Sartre

wrote the majority of "Being and Nothingness" there, his key philosophical work, by using the scenes around him to illustrate his abstract ideas. Simone de Beauvoir and Boris Vian also wrote in *Café de Flore,* while Pablo Picasso and Marc Chagall could often be found there engrossed in heated debates on art or scribbling quick sketches on the café's serviettes.

In Italy, it was *Caffé Greco* near the Spanish Steps in Rome, established in 1760, and the above-mentioned *Caffé Florian* in Venice, to which Europe's artists and intellectuals paid a visit on their obligatory trip around Italy. Goethe and Lord Byron, Casanova and Marcel Proust, Baudelaire and Gogol were guests here, as were Richard Wagner, Felix Mendelssohn-Bartholdy, Mark Twain, Thomas Mann and Ernest Hemingway. In Spain, Barcelona and Madrid were the centers of coffee house culture for painters and literary figures. Opened in 1916, *Cafe de Gijon* in Madrid, wreathed for many decades in a perpetual cloud of cigarette smoke, played host to José Ortega y Gasset, Federico García Lorca and Salvador Dalí, as well as Luis Buñuel and Fernando Arrabal from the 1920s onwards. In Lisbon, *Café a Brasileira*, with its large mirrors and carved ceilings was the regular haunt of the chain-smoking, absinthe-drinking poet Fernando Pessoa, whose bronze statue now stands in front of the café.

Café Slavia in Prague, opened in 1884, enjoyed particular literary esteem, remaining an "artists' café" in the 1930s style and playing host to intellectuals from Egon Erwin Kisch and the avant-garde literary circle to Václav Havel. Poems were dedicated to the café by Rainer Maria Rilke ("Café National") and Jaroslav Seifert ("Café Slavia"), a novel by Ota Filip ("Café Slavia", 1985), and a chapter in Reiner Kunze's "Wunderbaren Jahren" ("The Lovely Years"). In *Café Central* in Prague, young poets sat and talked with Rilke, Franz Kafka and Max Brod. Later, their café of choice became *Café Arco*, inspiring Karl Kraus' nickname for the group – "the Arconauts".

In the politically divided Germany of the 19th century, painters, poets and writers met in the coffee houses of the royal capitals, most notably Munich and Berlin – so many of them gathered in these cafés that Emanuel Geibel

left: Peter Altenberg at Café Central, 1907.
right: Today, cafés also serve as extended office space. St Oberholz in Berlin (left and above right) and Starbucks Coffee House (below right).

1907

Peter Altenberg im Café Central

spoke of the German coffee house as a "daycare center for smalltime authors". In Munich, the *Café Stadt München* and the *Café Dall'armi* were two of the gathering points for poets, while the group of painters known as the "Blauer Reiter" ("The Blue Rider") met in *Café Luitpold*, established in 1888. In 1920s Berlin the artistic and literary scene was centered on *Café Einstein*, once the villa of the silent movie star Henny Porten. A German coffee house that is especially rich in tradition is *Café Baum* in Leipzig, established under the name *Zum Arabischen Coffee Baum* in 1694. Among its regular guests were Richard Wagner and his father-in-law Franz Liszt, as well as the socialist leaders Wilhelm Liebknecht and August Bebel.

Many coffee houses in many different countries are today attempting to preserve or reinvigorate the tradition of the literary café. A modern example is the *Literaturhaus Café* in Hamburg, which was opened in 1989 and hosts regular book presentations and readings by authors from all over the world in a cozy coffee house ambience.

The Viennese Coffee House

By the end of the 19th century, Viennese coffee houses were widely acknowledged as the epitome of coffee house culture, an achievement in which the literary figures of the city's coffee houses played no small part. The very existence of the Viennese modern age, at its height between 1890 and 1914, and its various offshoots thereafter is simply unthinkable without the coffee house as a place for intellectual exchange. In 2011, this fact was acknowledged by UNESCO when it awarded the Viennese coffee house culture the status of World Heritage Site.

Just to name the numerous famous and richly traditional coffee houses and cafés in Vienna demands a book to itself. It is not only the many Viennese coffee creations and specialty cakes that define the Viennese coffee house culture, but also the tradition of serving coffee with a glass of tap water and the grumpy waiters with their curt remarks on current affairs and their inimitable blend of servility and arrogance. An array of endearing anecdotes circulate around the Viennese coffee houses, not all of

which can be verified, but are nevertheless wonderful tales. It is claimed, for example, that in early Viennese coffee houses, waiters came to the table with a color chart displaying shades from black to milky white, from which guests would choose the desired color of their coffee.

Around 25 famous Viennese coffee houses were designated artists' and writers' cafés, including *Café Griensteidl* (established 1844), the cafés *Herrenhof, Imperial, Museum, Sperl,* and particularly *Café Central*. While the sharp-tongued Karl Kraus and his eager followers gathered in *Café Imperial*, Hermann Broch, Franz Werfel, Robert Musil, Alfred Polgar and Egon Friedell met regularly in *Café Central* from 1910, where what became known as the "Mocha Symposium" assembled along with Franz Blei after the First World War. *Café Central* was the key case study in Alfred Polgar's essay on the coffee house as "Weltanschauung" ("world-view"): "*Café Central* is indeed a coffee house unlike any other. It is instead a world-view and one, to be sure, whose innermost essence is not to observe the world at all". In endearing images, Polgar describes the ivory tower mentality of many of the café's guests, who seek refuge from the uncertainties of life in the predictable, self-contained and inviting atmosphere of the coffee house.

Polgar voiced an aspect of the Viennese coffee house culture that is still prevalent among the city's literary cafés, that is a gathering place for bohemian and avant-garde figures, for libertines, misfits and artists. A significant number of the literary figures who populated the Viennese coffee houses were geniuses and mavericks who spent their time drinking coffee, reading newspapers and discussing ideas endlessly and who were simply unfit for ordered bourgeois life – figures like the occasional poet Peter Altenberg, or the melancholy romantic Joseph Roth, who swayed perilously between creative exuberance and depression. Even these burnt-out, anti-bourgeois geniuses found themselves at home in the atmosphere of a coffee house.

And today?

Laments about the end of the "real" coffee house are almost as old as the coffee house itself. Every change in taste and consumer demographic inspires woeful laments on the loss of the old and vocal assaults on the new as a sure sign of decay. After the end of the Second World War, cafés and coffee houses began to be displaced as sociable places by other institutions with more "character". Coffee too was no longer a luxury drink to be enjoyed in specialized surroundings, but became a standard feature in every household.

There are of course still traditional coffee houses in which guests can enjoy a coffee and a newspaper in relaxed surroundings, just as in previous centuries. At the same time, however, cafés and modern coffee shops since the 1980s – many of which belong to international chains – have been trying to respond to consumer demands in a hectic modern world, while also remaining true to the values of historic coffee house culture.

Coffee-drinking is certainly experiencing a powerful change of image and can no longer be perceived as a relaxing occupation for people who have too much time, but rather a means of fulfilling a need for busy people who no longer have any time at all. Modern coffee shops are therefore functional and clearly designed with large counters, where guests are offered unlimited variations on the content, size and aesthetics of their beverage. The interior is often more like a bar than a café, designed for people who will sit only briefly before moving on, drinking their coffee-to-go out of disposable paper cups with lids or taking it with them to drink on the move or in the office. Perhaps it is possible to say that while the ambience of coffee houses is in perpetual and unpredictable flux, the love of coffee among societies all over the world remains as strong as ever.

» Coffee should be black as Hell, strong as Death, and sweet as Love. «

Turkish proverb

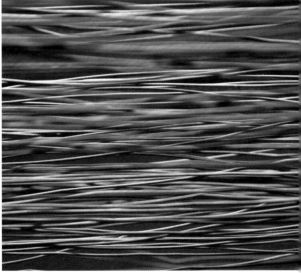

6T7 Espai Café

Girona, Spain

Architect: msb Estudi-Taller
Year of completion: 2011
Gross floor area: 100 m²
Materials: concrete and steel

The 6T7 Espai Café is far more than a place for serving coffee – it's a location for small gatherings, a space for exhibitions and a place where visitors can get close to architecture. Located in the old town with its stone gray tones, the café harmonizes perfectly with its surroundings with an empty, clean, sober interior. The entire container is finished with concrete, with the same strik-ing appearance and roughness as the street outside. Booths, bars and counter tops are constructed out of dramatic thick steel plates. One handmade piece – wire window panels filtering and blurring the light – human-izes the space, softening the severe interior. Sophistica-tion meets with bold simplicity in this arresting interior.

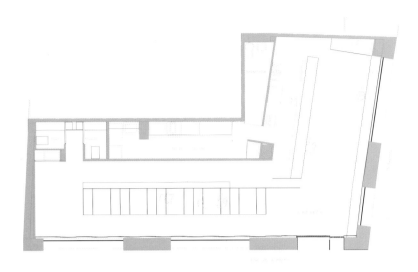

220 Grad

Salzburg, Austria

Architect: Riebenbauer Design / Franz Riebenbauer, Richy Oberriedmüller
Year of completion: 2008
Gross floor area: 220 m²
Materials: concrete, wood, glass

220 Grad is an architectural celebration of coffee – of its history, refinement and cultural significance through the ages. It is a sensual space in which coffee lovers can bask in the aromas and tastes of the highest quality coffee in the most sophisticated surroundings. Representing the natural origins of the humble coffee bean, the interior is constructed from simple materials – pure wood, pure concrete, pure glass – that gratify the eye without detracting from the café's central element: the coffee. A feast for all the senses, 220 Grad stands as a striking contemporary interpretation of a traditional Austrian roasting house and café.

Aroma Espresso Bar

New York, USA

Architect: Studio Gaia
Graphic Designer: Yotam Bezalel
Year of completion: 2009
Gross floor area: 319 m²
Materials: oak wood

Aroma Espresso Bar in 72nd Street, New York, is the second US branch of an Israeli café company. With vibrant colors, playful wall graphics and designer chairs styled for lingering, the two-level coffee house translates the concept for the company's original New York venue – a long, narrow Soho space with a huge window façade – to a completely different neighborhood vibe.

The material template starts with red wall tiles that arch down from the ceiling and extend the brand's modern yet homely ambience. Distinctive rhythmic arches, separated by niches that contain indirect lighting fixtures, are just one of many strong visual statements that give the space its dynamic, theatrical look, while also giving this stretch of 72nd Street some much-needed pizzazz.

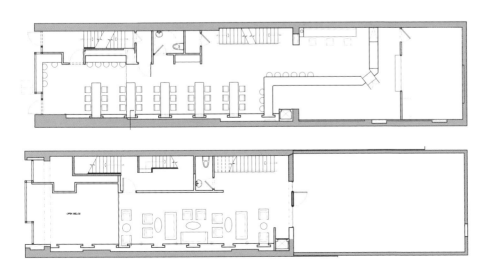

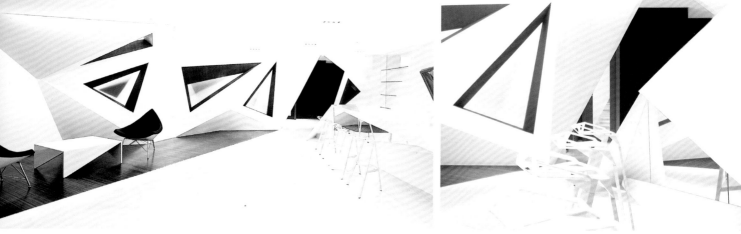

Arthouse Café

Hangzhou, China

Architect: Joey Ho Design
Other Designers: Yuki Leung, Momoko Lai
Year of completion: 2010
Gross floor area: 279 m²
Materials: stone, wood, corian

Serving coffee in the daytime and alcohol at night, Arthouse Café provides visitors with a fresh dynamic ambience within an exhibition gallery. Inspired by basic geometry, a single triangular form presented in various dimensions and at various angles dominates the space, exploding the boundary between traditionally divided units, such as the wall, floor and ceiling. As visitors move through the space, they are met with radical and unexpected geometric contexts at every turn. Minimal materials such as timber, artificial white marble and Corian combine with basic geometric shapes to create an unprecedented interior that challenges the senses and reinvigorates the soul.

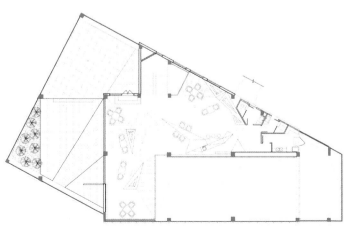

Bea's of Bloomsbury at One New Change

London, United Kingdom

Architect: carbon
Year of completion: 2010
Gross floor area: 110 m²

Representing modern design with an aesthetic twist inspired by Japanese tea houses, this new café adjacent to St Paul's Cathedral is the second location of Bea's of Bloomsbury, an independent boutique café. The unique and experiential interior space reflects the same care and passion that Bea has for the food she serves – both the stunning architecture and the delectable food

are expressions of her singular identity. A dark neutral background allows the cupcakes to take centre stage in their individual glass display boxes, while lighting is kept ambient with a soft comfortable glow from the ceramic teapot lights suspended at various heights. At night, the display boxes and teapot lights exude a welcoming glow that brightens the face of every passerby.

Breeze Café

Las Vegas, USA

Architect: GRAFT
Year of completion: 2010

The Aria Pool Deck, Restaurant and Bar are situated in the spectacular City Center complex of hotels, residences, casinos, spas and retail areas. Comprising an intimate sanctuary of cabanas around a luscious pool, this project represents a welcome haven of calm in a hectic urban environment. The structures constitute a fusion of the stunning beauty and richness of the tropics and the simplicity of contemporary culture. Comprising a superbly designed series of overlapping contours, envisioned as a metaphor of fluidity and a means to establish a spatial hierarchy for the distinct lounge areas, the architecture is bold and highly innovative. Massaranduba wood and a rich array of textiles were chosen for their simplicity, beauty and cultural significance.

Café Angelikahöhe

Schwarzenberg, Austria

Architect:
Michael Ohneberg Architektur
Year of completion: 2008
Gross floor area: 155 m²
Materials: silver fir, maple,
oak wood

Café Angelikahöhe has long resided at the center of the Bregenz café culture. Now newly restored, it has once again become a wonderfully cozy meeting place for locals and guests alike, for young and old. With a closed back wall and a façade open to the natural landscape, this café is uniquely designed to offer each and every visitor the experience they are seeking – whether a brief respite from a frantic outside world or a joyous interaction with the stunning Bregenz forests. New facing made from the pale wood of silver fir trees combines with maple flooring to construct the space and guide the visitor's eye towards the green meadows beyond the café's walls. Chairs and tables were stained dark to generate a contrast with the pale walls that is stark and evocative.

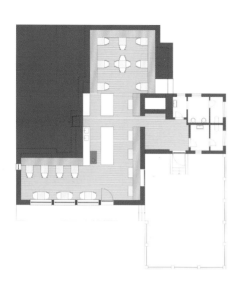

Café Coutume

Paris, France

Architect: CUT architectures
Year of completion: 2011
Gross floor area: 90 m²
Materials: tiles, oak wook,
PVC, glass

Café Coutume combines a coffee roastery with a café in a space that fuses Parisian chic with the feel of a laboratory – a radical yet evocative juxtaposition. Coffee culture has been redefined in this café in the center of Paris through the installation of high-end tools and machines. Tearing down the walls and ceilings restored a stunning Parisian interior with high ceilings, mouldings, columns and an old shop door. The Parisian atmosphere

is perfected by the addition of new oak flooring. Square white tiles, grid lighting, stainless steel, industrial plastic curtains and laboratory glassware create the impression of a laboratory of coffee, a place where experimentation meets relaxation. Cut Architectures have blended tradition, alchemy and technique to create a unique experience for the coffee lover.

Café del Arco

Murcia, Spain

Architect: Clavel Arquitectos
Year of completion: 2009
Gross floor area: 189 m²
Materials: irokowood strips over a galvanized and lacquered steel framework

The principle of "architecture in interior" rather than "interior design" inspired the architects of Café del Arco. Asked to redesign an existing café, they used a winding cul-de-sac layout as a leitmotif to connect the heterogeneous interior elements. Starting from the façade, a continuous vertical-lines surface made of warm iroko wood strips wraps the building, embracing it while barely touching it, before turning inside, organizing circulation and sitting spaces, gracefully tracing the shape of the bar and quietly returning to the façade where it began. The floor in the bar space is paved with stone from a local quarry, echoing the public pavement outside the building, while a vegetation-like carpet covering the walls on the upper floor celebrates the relationship of interior with exterior, epitomized by the elegant wooden strip that traverses conventional architectural boundaries.

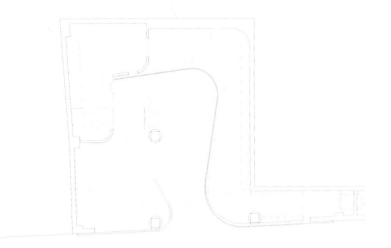

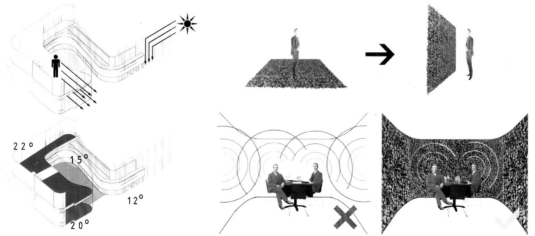

Café Foam

Stockholm, Sweden

Architect: Note Design Studio
Year of completion: 2011
Gross floor area: 180 m²
Materials: wood, concrete

Asked to create an interior "that people either love or hate and that nobody is indifferent to", Note design studio began this project by searching for a suitable inspiration. The spectacular result is an interior inspired by bullfighting, a sport that never fails to arouse the extremes of passion and hate. The constant, dance-like struggle between man and bull is manifested in the design concept, as are the dazzling materials and colors found in bullfighting arenas. Allowing the feisty Spanish temperament to meet Scandinavian coolness, the designers created a vivid space that provokes and inspires without overwhelming the visitor, and dramatically enhances the gastronomic experience.

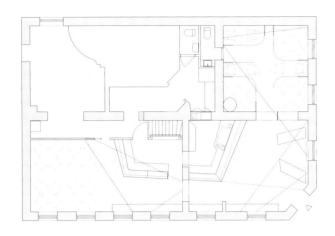

FOAM 11

COFFEEBAR&CAFÉ
QUALITY&WELFARE
FRESHFOOD&DRINKS
LOVE&UNDERSTANDING
SOFT&HARD&SOFTAGAIN
OPENWEEKDAYS

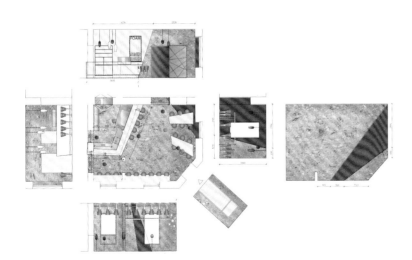

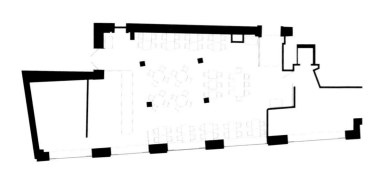

Café Liberty

London, United Kingdom

Architect: SHH
Year of completion: 2011
Gross floor area: 125 m²

SHH have revamped Café Liberty, the 60-cover, second floor restaurant at London's iconic Liberty department store on Regent Street, originally constructed in 1924. The fast-turnaround, tight-budget project has radically changed the look and feel of the space, re-integrating it into the style and spirit of the original Arts & Crafts building, thanks to a number of choice vintage and contemporary interventions. Major new features include stunning reclaimed 1920s doors; a 1920s Arts & Crafts washstand, reading desk and mahogany cabinet to serve as greeter and waiter stations; eye-catching hand-blocked wallpaper, and three neon flying ducks at the entrance of the café, lending the room a surprising contemporary twist.

Café Sonja/temporary café

Vienna, Austria

Architect: Postlerferguson
Year of completion: 2011
Gross floor area: 83 m²
Materials: MDF, mylar, leather, ceramic tiles

Designed for the 2011 Vienna Design Week, this glamorous temporary café draws on the unique aesthetics and feel of a traditional Viennese coffee house. The architects created a space dominated by dark colors, intriguing interlocking structures and highly reflective gold surfaces. These combine to create a mysterious atmosphere evocative of the mythical setting of the Brothers' Grimm compelling fairytales. Mylar covered wing-like structures reflect the light from the ceiling, generating a glowing effect that enhances the sense of the surreal. Café Sonja's fleeting existence – constructed in two days and operational for a single week – means that it is preserved only in the memories of the lucky few who spent time there, perhaps appropriate for such an otherworldly space.

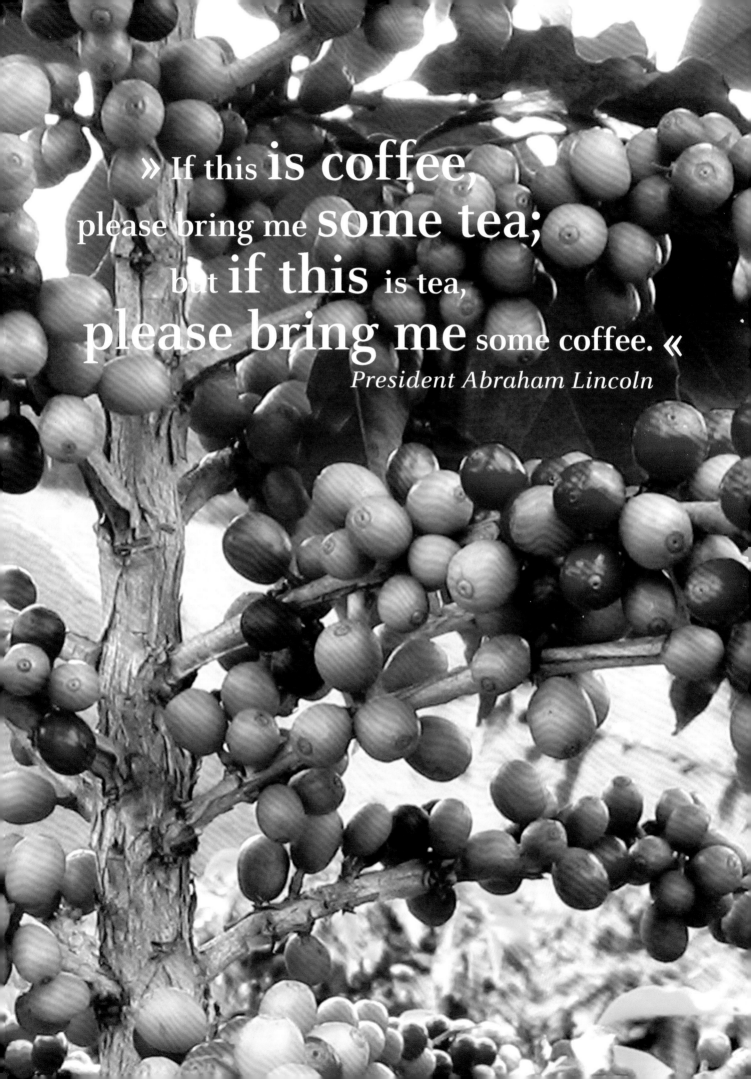

» If this **is coffee,** please bring me **some tea;** but **if this** is tea, **please bring me** some coffee. «

President Abraham Lincoln

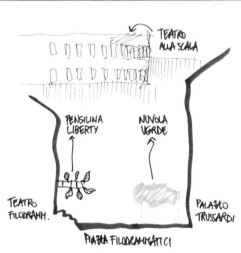

TEATRO
ALLA SCALA

PENSILINA
LIBERTY

NUVOLA
VERDE

TEATRO
FILODRAMM.

PALAZZO
TRUSSARDI

PIAZZA FILODRAMMATICI

Café Trussardi

Milan, Italy

Architect: carlorattiassociati |
walter nicolino & carlo ratti
Interior Design: David Drago
Vertical Greenery:
Patrick Blanc
Year of completion: 2008
Gross floor area: 60 m²

This extension of the café on the ground floor of a Milanese fashion house represents a wholly new architectural venture. Acting as a glass case, the new terrace is dominated by the real hanging garden suspended from the roof, an astonishing feature made possible thanks to the "Mur Végetal" invented by French botanist Patrick Blanc. 120 different plant species have been cleverly placed on the thin support structure, creating the dramatic effect of a green cloud floating in space, breathing life into the café below. Visitors are absorbed into an organic world, where architecture has given way to the beauty of nature. Beneath this living canopy is a flaneur's paradise, where beautiful leather-covered Panton chairs invite total relaxation.

Cafeteria Rog

Ljubljana, Slovenia

Architect: Špela Leskovic and Aleš Košak / AKSL arhitekti
Graphic Design: Saša Kerkoš and Dani Bajc;
Industrial Design: Studio Drevo – Dejan Pfifer
Year of completion: 2010
Gross floor area: 130
Materials: ceramics, oak, wood, leather, copper, kerrock

Located in an ancient building with a vaulted ceiling and old arched windows, New Cafeteria Rog offers stunning views onto the river Ljubljanica. In the café's interior, the local past is carefully preserved and juxtaposed with contemporary accents, while bright and dark tones of wood and leather mingle in perfect harmony. Echoes of the nearby former factory Rog, which produced bicycles for many years, emanate from a piece of wall art with a fantasy bicycle graphic and a wall providing information about the history of the local area. Copper shades evoke memories of copper pots filled with aromatic Turkish coffee, while hexagonal ceramic tiles with subtle 3D decoration pave the floors and parts of the walls. Extended ceiling lights allow private ambient lighting above the tables, each of which is positioned in a unique, intimate space.

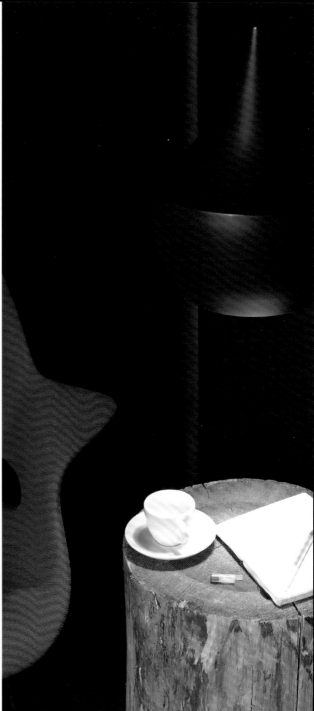

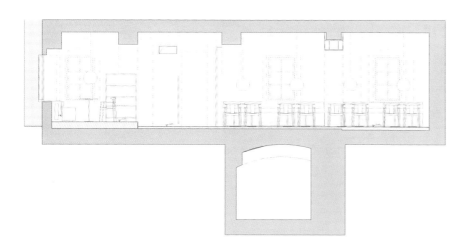

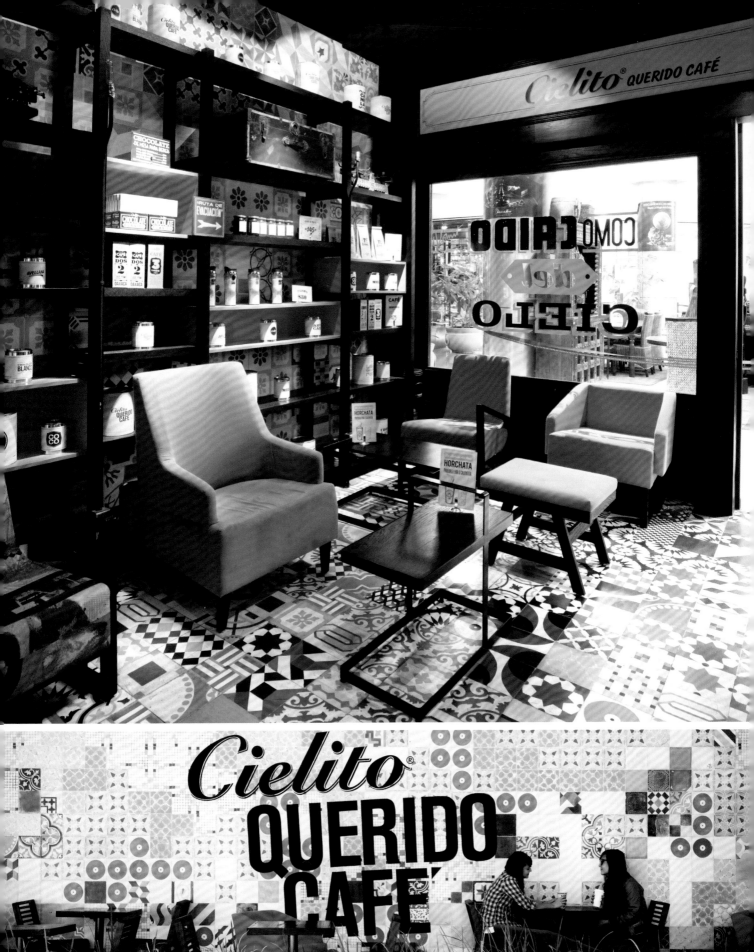

Cielito Querido Café

Mexico City, Mexico

Architect: Esrawe / Cadena+Asociados Branding
Other creatives: Rocio Serna, Joaquin Ceballos
Year of completion: 2010
Materials: recovered wood, tiles

Cielito Querido Café is a Latin American reinvention of the coffeehouse experience. It is a place that surprises, confronts and engages all senses through its space, aroma, taste, color and history. Drawing their inspiration from Mexican history, the designers incorporated the joyful colors, symbolic language and illustrated graphics of the late 19th to early 20th century into the strik-ing interior. The Latin American sign-maker's trade is celebrated through the display of product labels from old grocery and general stores, generating an evocative graphic language belonging to a culture that is spec-tacularly rich in history. In this unique space, however, that past has been radically reinvented in a joyful, poetic, nostalgic celebration of contemporary Mexican life.

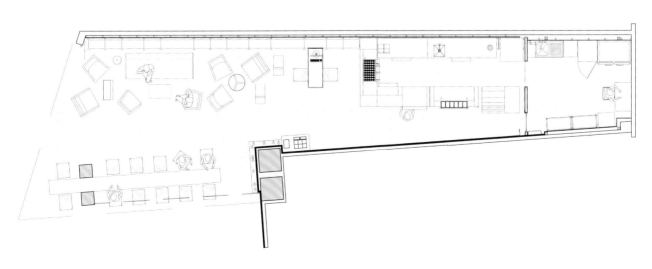

Dekko Café

New York, USA

Architect: Antonio Di Oronzo/bluarch architecture + interiors + lighting
Year of completion: 2010
Gross floor area: 1,115 m²
Materials: reflective chrome ceiling, rustic birch wood walls, frosted acrylic fins, polished concrete floor, and fire-rated vinyl upholstered banquettes.

Passers-by stop and gaze at Dekko Café, a new venue that offers a casual, yet unique dining experience in a setting that invites interaction with the world outside. Expansive and frameless operable window systems, which fold neatly to reveal the simple wall openings, are the essence and origin of the café's name – "Dekko", a British idiom for "look". This refreshing openness is continued in the design of the interior, which takes its cues from the urban life on the doorstep – both in the reflective chromed ceiling above the bar and the walls and ceilings, clad in rustic birch to add a welcome warmth to this modern space. Frosted, semicircular Plexiglas profiles attached to the ceiling further soften the atmosphere.

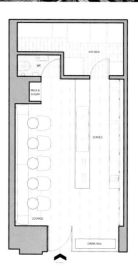

D'Espresso
New York, USA

Architect: nemaworkshop
Year of completion: 2010
Gross floor area: 39 m²
Materials: tiles, wood, glass

Located on Madison Avenue, this innovative espresso bar conceptually and literally turns a normal room sideways, creating a striking identity for the emerging D'Espresso brand. Inspired by the nearby Bryant Park Library, nemaworkshop designed an interior that follows the simple, yet novel, principle of taking a library and turning it sideways. The booklined shelves become the floor and ceilings, and wood flooring ends up on the walls, while pendants protrude sideways. The frosted glass wall behind the service counter illuminates the space, and the wall directly opposite is richly clad in dark brown herringbone. If somewhat unnerving at first, this bold interior challenges each visitor to question their perspective on a world that is not always what it seems.

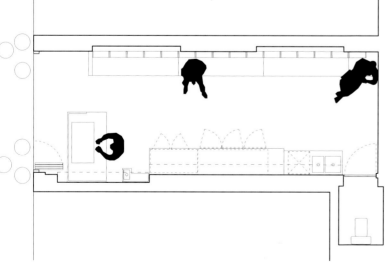

Detour Espresso Bar

Darlinghurst, Australia

Architect: Rory The Architect
Year of completion: 2008
Gross floor area: 30 m²
Materials: plywood, stainless steel, pressed metal

With a small space, a short timeframe and a modest budget, Rory The Architect has achieved wonders at the Detour Espresso Bar. The long narrow space is divided lengthwise with seating on one side and preparation space opposite, each complementing the other. A dramatic plywood joiner wall serves a host of purposes – it conceals light fittings, provides storage and softens the space acoustically, as well as providing a bold yet simple visual focus for the interior. Structural plywood and stainless steel speak of utility and toughness, while the bright green forest walls and ceiling provide a delightfully fresh counterpoint to the urban atmosphere. This quirky oasis of calm offers a welcome refuge for locals and travellers alike in an otherwise hectic city.

Di Più

Vienna, Austria

Architect: Kohlmayr Lutter Knapp | Office for Systemic Design
Floor picture: Luzia Ellert
Year of completion: 2010
Gross floor area: 250 m²

Located in an area of great architectural spectacle and flamboyance, Di Più represents a refreshingly modest approach to café design. The design is modest and unassuming, allowing the visitors and the food to take precedence. The new skin – the visible layer – is constructed from low-cost materials that are not often seen in gastronomic settings. Subject to highly innovative modifications, however, these raw materials have acquired new and vibrant characteristics that lend the space a unique, yet still understated, personality. Unconventional illumination features and simple furnishings enrich that quirky identity.

Dishoom

London, United Kingdom

Architect: Afroditi Krassa
Year of completion: 2010
Gross floor area: 465 m²
Materials: tiles, oak panelling, white Carrara marble topped tables

In 2008, three entrepreneurs came to Afroditi with a simple but challenging brief – to design a contemporary Indian restaurant that avoids clichés and stereotypes: this was to be something new and wholly unexpected. And so the Dishoom identity was born. Drawing on Bombay's rich past and the honest, resourceful and functional interiors that have developed throughout its history, the interiors combine elegant, sophisticated and simple lines with art deco influences. Checkerboard tiles, oak panelling, white Carrara marble and mismatched chairs create a relaxed and democratic space, while a compelling monochromatic color palette compliments retro Bombay portraiture and 1960s pop imagery perfectly.

RULES OF THE CAFE

NO SMOKING
NO FIGHTING
NO CREDIT
NO FOOD FROM OUTSIDE
NO TALKING LOUD
NO SPITTING
NO BARGAINING
NO CHEATING
NO WATER TO OUTSIDERS
NO MATCHES
NO GAMBLING
NO COMBING HAIR
ALL CASTES WELCOME

El Portillo

Teruel, Spain

Architect: Stone Designs
Year of completion: 2010
Gross floor area: 80 m²
Materials: wood, textiles

The architects of El Portillo jumped at the chance to create a hamburger café in a wooden cabin nestled in a snowy landscape at the Javalambre ski station in Teruel, Spain. Their key idea was to create an interior and exterior that would co-exist harmoniously and complement each other visually. The exterior was painted black and decorated with illustrations of mythical creatures, creating a dramatic and eye-catching contrast with the snowy landscape. The interior, on the other hand, mimics the white landscape, with vibrant color added through bright red climbing ropes and green felt panels. Even on cloudy days, El Portillo provides a cozy space in which to take refuge during the harshest days of winter.

Everyday Chaa

Seoul, South Korea

Architect: MAEZM +
Sarah Kim
Year of completion: 2011
Gross floor area: 208 m²
Materials: wood flooring,
painting

Seoul, a city saturated with cafés, has recently gained a spectacular new addition to its tea-drinking culture, a space where consumption can be enjoyed in clean, modern and friendly surroundings. Sleek and sophisticated, the monochrome walls graduate from white near the ceiling to black near the floor. Merging effortlessly with the tops of the walls, the ceiling and exposed struc-

tural elements have been finished in white. Curved white sculptures are suspended from the ceiling, drawing the visitor's eye with their enthralling shape and luminosity. The timber flooring is painted black, blending with the base of the walls. Everyday Chaa represents the ultimate in café elegance and refinement.

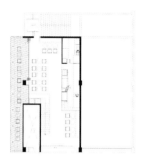

94

EVERYDAY
CHAA

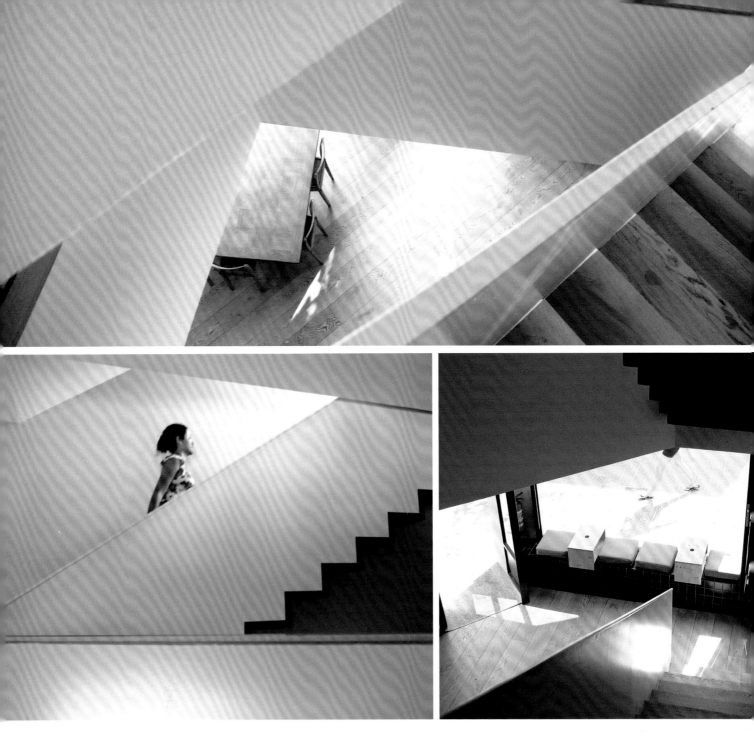

Federal Café

Barcelona, Spain

Architect: Barbara Appolloni
Interior design: Christopher King, Tommy Tang
Year of completion: 2010
Gross floor area: 260 m²

This charmingly cozy, informal café/bistro with an Australian touch is perfectly in tune with its owners' origins. Although the façade has been restored with minimal intervention, to remain in keeping with neighboring buildings, the woodwork has been ingeniously designed so that the interior remains open to the street. Retractable steel shutters and a stunning bench clad in black ceramic tiles mark the permeable boundary between interior and exterior. Entering the café, the visitor's eye is drawn up the dramatic concrete steps to the upper floor where the ambience becomes more intimate, the architecture ever more compelling.

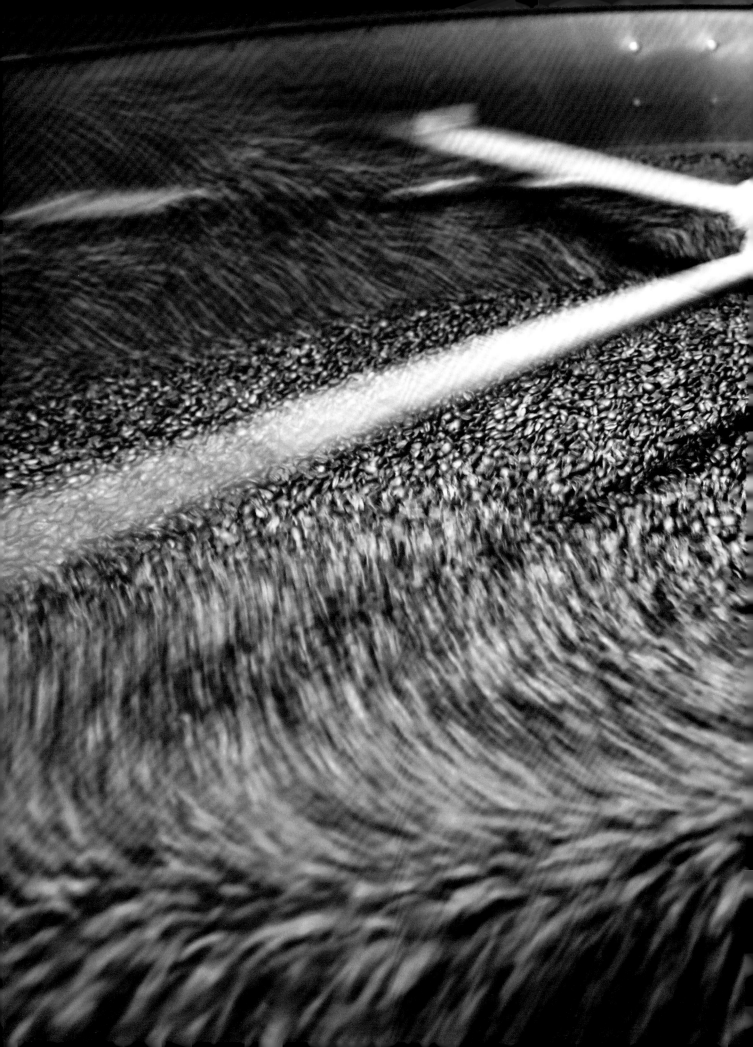

» There are **two things** that are **difficult** to come by in **the** Vatican: honesty and a **cup of coffee.** «

Pope John Paul I

Fonte Cafe and Wine Bar

Seattle, USA

Architect: Floisand Studio
Murals: Somelab Design
Year of completion: 2009
Gross floor area: 167 m²
Materials: caesarstone, milestone, blackened steel, fir, glass

Nestled at the base of Seattle's Four Seasons Hotel, the Fonte Café and Wine Bar is Fonte's highly impressive flagship café and retail store. Initially presented with design challenges including low ceilings, exposed piping and limited natural light, the architects have fashioned a highly sophisticated interior that will charm every coffee lover. The dining spaces are marked by a series of rough-sawn fir soffits that house subtle lighting, hide utilities and float unobtrusively above the built-in banquettes. A colonnade of curvy steel columns intersect the wood soffits, gently guiding the customer from the entry to a brightly-lit bar. Sleek, white counters and a glowing glass backsplash showcase the café's menu, coffee and extensive wine collection.

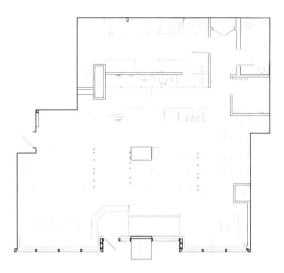

Frans Hals Museum Café

Haarlem, The Netherlands

Architect: Maurice Mentjens
Wall artwork: XY dumb-
office 2002 Jean-Pierre
Zoetbrood
Year of completion: 2009
Gross floor area: 200 m²

The design of this elegant café uniquely honors the sober yet sophisticated "schutterstukken" (group portraits of civilian guards) by the Dutch master of painting, Frans Hals. Each house in the row of three has been given its own color palette in elegant shades of gray. Orange, white and blue – the colors of the historical Dutch flag – provide vibrant, yet subtle accents. The architect honors the sober, minimalistic, underlit qualities of Hals' paintings, all of which have been lovingly replicated in the café's interior design. The result is a spectacular three-dimensional deconstruction and transmutation of a sumptuous "schutterstuk" from the Golden Age of Dutch history. In this café, the enjoyment of coffee is inextricably interwoven with the enjoyment of art.

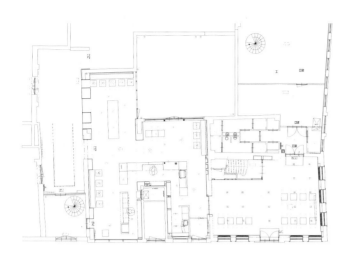

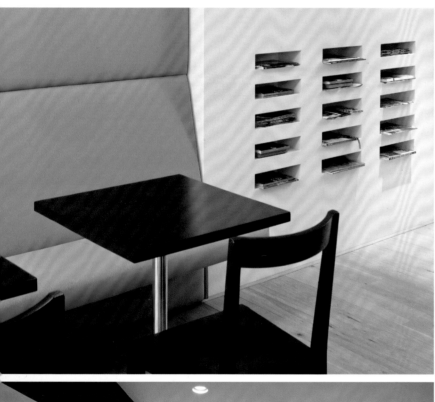

Grand Cafe Usine

Eindhoven, The Netherlands

Architect: Bearandbunny
Year of completion: 2009
Gross floor area: 1000 m²

The former Philips light tower is now host to Grand Café Usine, based on the ground floor of the iconic building. Designed according to the concept "A grand café for everyone", every feature from the menu to the décor reflects that powerful unifying principle. The bold juxtaposition of a contemporary, stylish interior with a derelict, functional building has resulted in a stunning space that celebrates the architectural possibilities of unifying the old and the new, the past and the present. Tiled floors and bare concrete walls act as a canvas of possibility, to which brightly colored chairs, benches and an eclectic array of lamps were added. The tables were inspired by old sewing machine tables, while the seating comprises a mixture of classic designs and repainted antiques.

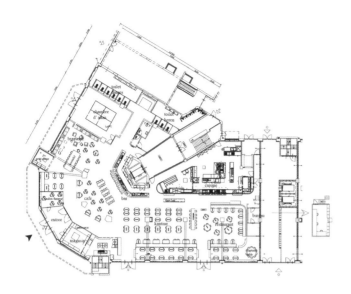

Intelligentsia Coffee

Venice, USA

Architect: MASS Architecture, Design, Build
Year of completion: 2009
Gross floor area: 186 m²
Materials: metal, wood, glass

Intelligentsia Coffee presented the architects with an apparently simple request: a coffee house that showcased the coffee-making process without using any of the standard elements of coffee-house design. In a radical departure from the conventional café concept, the architects decided to remove the counter – the barrier between barista and customer. Instead, they created a series of self-contained stations, one for each barista, making the process of serving coffee wonderfully fluid and flexible. Three basic materials – metal, wood and glass – divide the interior effectively into preparation, display and mechanical areas. This is less of a café and more of a coffee factory, a space where architectural innovation has triumphed.

113

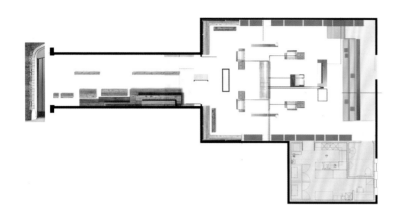

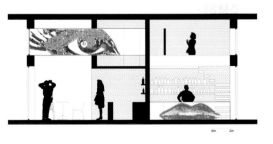

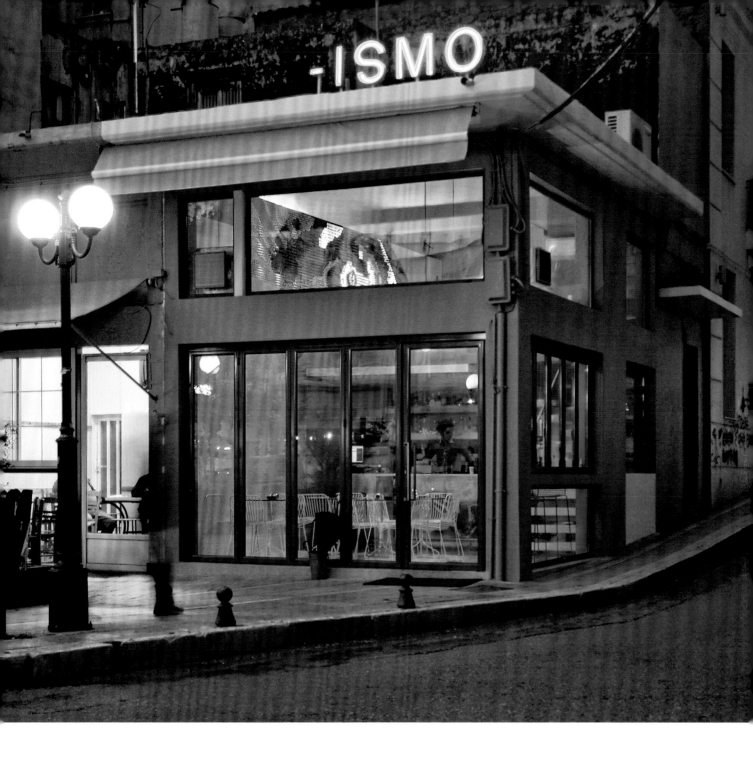

Ismo

Agrinio, Greece

Architect: Point Supreme
Architects & John Karahalos
Year of completion: 2009
Gross floor area: 20 m²
Materials: aluminium, plaster-
board, wallpaper

Inspired by a series of radical art movements, their
Greek names ending in "-ismo", Point Supreme installed
a series of spectacular and audacious installations on
the perpendicular walls of this café. A giant eye and
mouth combine to appear as a cubist face, dominat-
ing the space. During the day, it appears as a simple
painting with the soft, earthy tones of a Rousseau
landscape. As day turns to night, the eye is transformed
into a sensual illumination with vibrant, engrossing
colors. Thousands of tiny holes allow light to penetrate
the aluminium surface of the eye, which seems to wink
enticingly from every angle. The neutral white of the rest
of the café only heightens the intensity of these unique
pieces of art.

Kith Café

Singapore

Architect: HJGHER
Year of completion: 2009
Gross floor area: 28 m²
Materials: plywood, iron

Inspired by the simple phrase, "Would you care to have coffee with me sometime?", this is a café with the power to turn strangers into kith and kin. Open wrought-iron shelves, a handwritten menu on a dusty chalkboard and naked light bulbs emphasize Kith's ethos of sincerity, openness and simplicity. Elegant custom-made furniture for the seating area was designed to be flexible, to break down personal space barriers and encourage customers to interact. These striking modular blocks were hand-crafted from 10,000 blocks of plywood, trimmed to varying lengths and thicknesses before being hand-layered. The individuality of each block evokes the random, organic growth of the trees from which they came and celebrates a natural world that makes architecture possible.

Koeppe Jemp

Hoscheid-Dickt, Luxembourg

Architect: modulor menuiserie + design
Year of completion: 2011
Gross floor area: 90 m²
Material: massive oak wood, schist, rusty metal elements, white painted surface and the old mosaic floor

The architects of this stunning project aimed to preserve the building's past, while developing a wholly contemporary space suitable for a 21st century clientele. Massive oak, schist and rusty elements were chosen as the key materials with which this modernization could be realized. The combination of authentic, untreated materials with a simple contemporary design has generated a striking interior perfectly suited to a modern audience. The original rustic character of the space has been maintained through the preservation of the original mosaic floor and the addition of a Memory Wall, which displays historic images of the café and its founder, Koeppe Jemp. Diffused lighting emanating from self-made lamps perfects this cozy, timeless café.

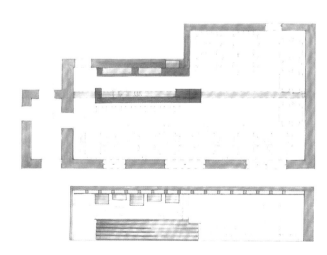

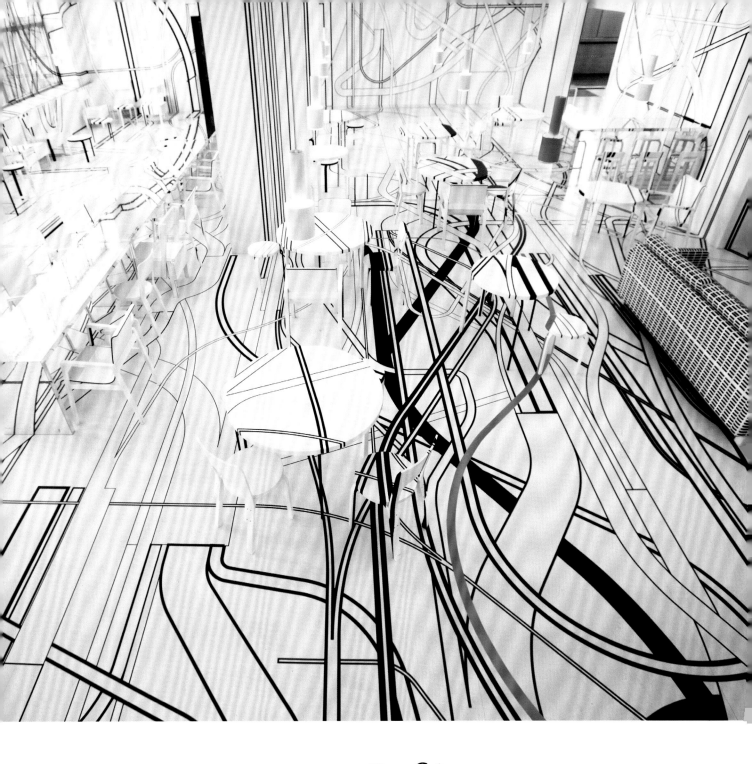

Logomo Café
Turku, Finland

Architect: Tobias Rehberger/
Artek
Year of completion: 2010
Gross floor area: 230 m²

This comprehensive art installation at the Logomo Café was designed by German artist Tobias Rehberger in collaboration with Artek. Intrigued by the concept of a visual art project which was about "not seeing something", Rehberger created a dazzling space which both draws the eye and disguises what is actually there. The white interior is adorned with bold black graphic lines that flow randomly over the surfaces, ceaselessly overlapping and intertwining with one another. The simple white Artek furniture is absorbed into the artwork – chairs and tables are simply continuations of walls and floors – while a single orange lamp and single orange line represent a daring intrusion of color into this intoxicating space.

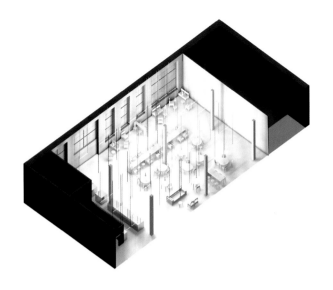

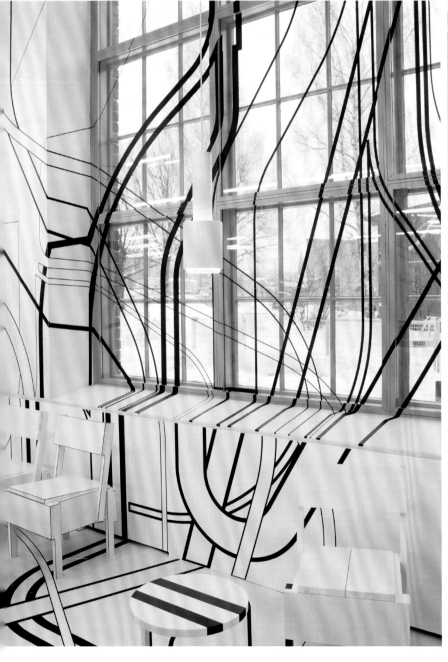

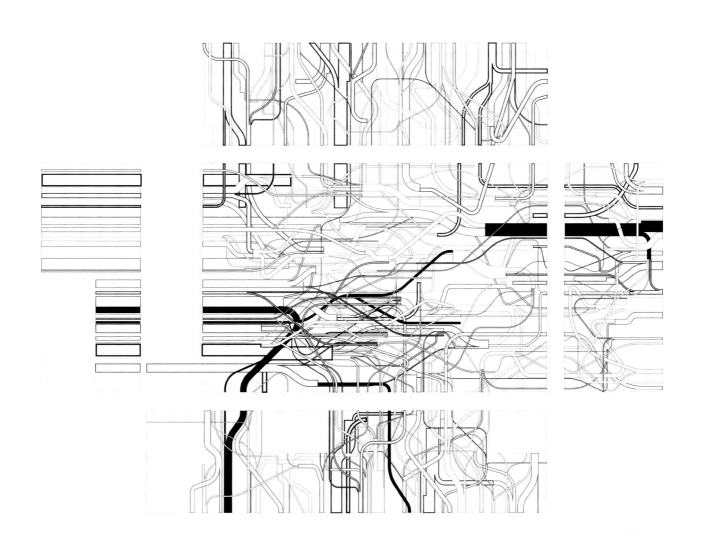

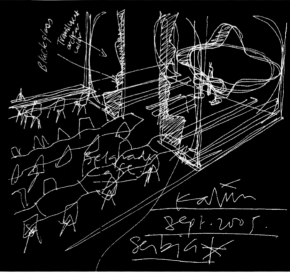

Majik Café

Belgrade, Serbia

Architect: Karim Rashid
Year of completion: 2008
Gross floor area: 136 m²
Materials: stainless steel,
vinyl, glass, leather, lime

Majik Café stems from Karim Rashid's philosophy of creating a digital space and a seamless world that excites all the senses. Karim Rashid's love of sensuous lines and brilliant hues comes through gloriously in the dynamic space. A scrolling LED message board displays customers' text messages, while a vibrant patterned glass bar changes color and mood throughout the day.

The exterior is finished strikingly in polished stainless steel and mosaic tile. Icon-shaped windows and decorative ancient Serbian patterns are impressively updated to create a kaleidoscopic, engaging and inspiring fulgent space for lounging, dining and drinking. The message is of east-meets-west digital freedom, where technology and social networking are absorbed and celebrated.

Mazzo

Amsterdam, The Netherlands

Architect: concrete
Year of completion: 2010
Gross floor area: 400 m²
Materials: concrete, brickwork, stone, pinewood, steel

Situated in a typical Amsterdam building, characterized by narrow, deep spaces, Mazzo represents a radical experiment in the design of a gastronomic interior. The first section, with its five-meter high ceiling, is perfect for a bar, cozily lit with wall lights and suspension lights to create a living room ambience. A few original stone columns divide the second section into two zones, housing a kitchen and a seating area that is stunningly lit with modern chandeliers. Mazzo's evocative visual identity arises from the raw, honest interior, constructed from a compelling juxtaposition of concrete, brickwork, stone, pinewood and raw steel. Clear shapes, grids and high-contrast black-and-white images generate a distinct graphic identity.

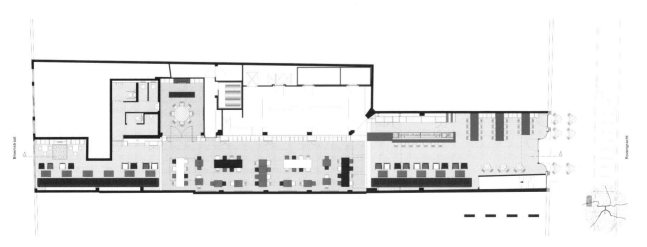

McNally Jackson Cafe

New York, USA

Architect: Front Studio
Architects
Year of completion: 2010
Gross floor area: 56 m²

Located in a large independent bookshop in downtown Manhattan, the McNally Jackson Café has been redesigned along a literary theme. The result of a wonderfully fluid collaboration between the owner and architects, all of them avid readers, the newly realized space generates endlessly evocative connections to the act of reading. A scattering of books hangs precipitously from the ceiling, as if thrown joyously into the sky and frozen. The wallpaper covering the curved wall around the seating area is fashioned entirely out of open spine books – the texture of the print creates a rippling effect, powerfully evoking movement and restlessness. The simple joy of a good book and a good coffee is celebrated in the very essence of this literary café.

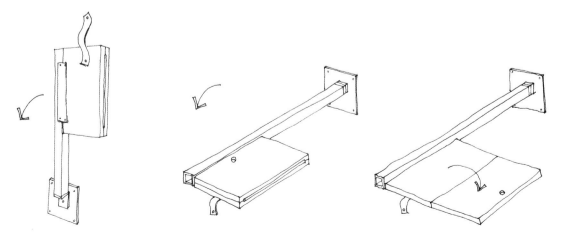

» Coffee **doesn't dehydrate** the body. If it did, I'd already be a **pile of dust.** «

Franz Kafka

Meltino Bar & Lounge

Braga, Portugal

Architect: Architect Claudia Costa / Studio LOFF Architecture and Lighting Design
Year of completion: 2010
Gross floor area: 182 m²
Materials: MDF, pinewood, linoleum

The simple concept of a café embedded in a shopping center is taken to a radical new level by Meltino Bar & Lounge. Claudia Costa aimed to create a space that would endure in the visual memory of every visitor, and she has achieved that aim in spectacular style. The idea was to represent coffee beans in geometric forms, replacing the commercial context of the café with a coffee grain that pierces walls, roofs and counters to both construct and embrace the interior. Shadows cast by the pinewood structure are interspersed with dancing spots of brightness – an intoxicating play of light and dark. Lighting provided by diachronic and halogen lamps creates a surreal space in which the outside world simply to ceases to exist.

meltino bar & lounge

um café feito de café

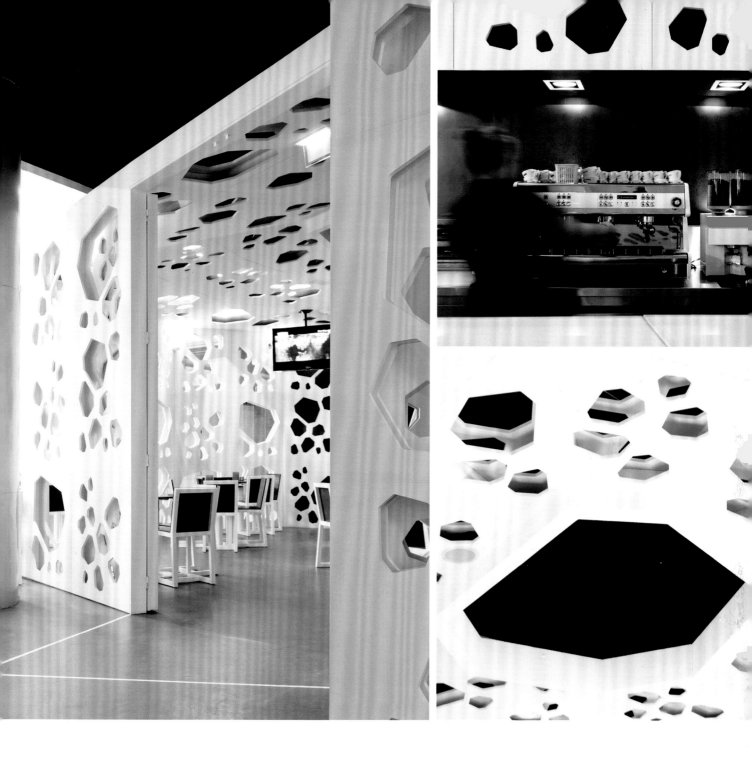

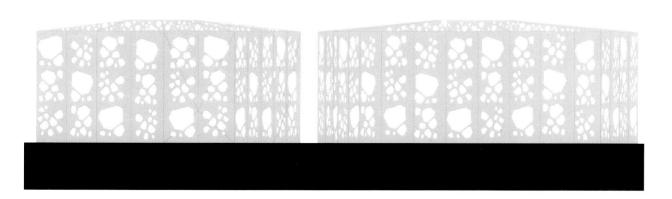

Mishi Blyachera Café

Dnipropetrovs'ka, Ukraine

Architect: Studio Belenko
Year of completion: 2007
Gross floor area: 225 m²

The vintage interior of Mishi Blyachera establishes a sense of timelessness: this café's interior seems a world away from the bustle of 21st century life on the doorstep outside. Painstakingly assembled and breathtakingly detailed, every element of the interior contributes to its homely atmosphere, from the soft brown cushions to the sepia photographs and retro lampshades. Studio

Balenko more than compensated for their modest budget in the time and effort spent in creating this charmingly cluttered space where nothing is exactly what it seems: books are stacked to act as furniture while glass bottles function as vases. To step inside is to be absorbed, for a brief while, into a comforting past.

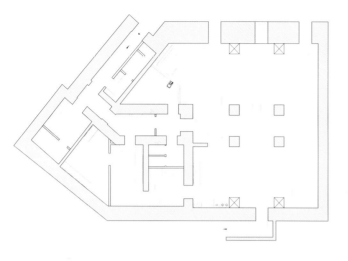

Mocha Mojo

Chennai, India

Architect: mancini enterprises
Year of completion: 2010
Gross floor area: 350 m²
Materials: MDF, acrylic emulsion paint, industrial self leveling resin floor, upholstery canvas

This vast coffee house in Chennai was inspired by the architecture of the 1960s and 1970s when opulence and ornament dominated design. These principles have been dramatically infused into the interiors of Mocha Mojo in a glorious celebration of intense color and shape. Lego-like blocks of varying sizes and shapes are stacked along the walls, protruding at unexpected angles to create a series of unique spaces. Up to 110 visitors can enjoy the café at any one time, a colorful space in which childhood memories can be revived and wonderful new memories created.

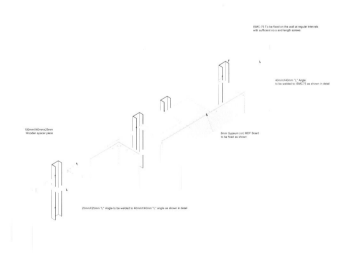

Muzeum Sztuki Café

Lódz, Poland

Architect: Paulina Stepień,
Magdalena Koziej –
Wunderteam
Year of completion: 2009
Gross floor area: 315 m²
Material: plywood, metal,
glass

Drawing inspiration both from the avant-garde tradition and the building's historic function, Polish design studio Wunderteam created a striking interior for this café on the ground floor of the Muzeum Sztuki in Lodz. Simple materials – plywood, metal and glass – have been fashioned and fused in unique ways to create a stunning space dominated by unusual geometry. Reminiscent of a forgotten art warehouse – with mobile furniture styled as transport crates, carts and platforms – the architecture references and celebrates its cultural context. The bar, an evocative crystalline form of plywood and acrylic glass, seems to grow out of the floor and walls, a fragment of a mysterious, intriguing sculpture. In this space, the perfect fusion of art, architecture and beauty can be discovered and explored.

153

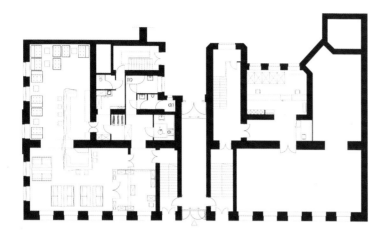

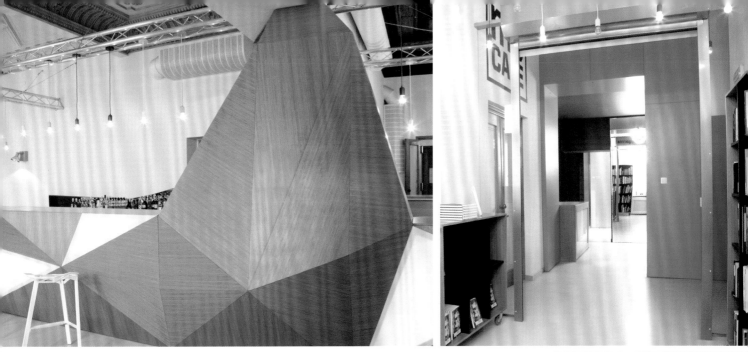

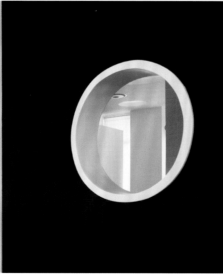

Petit Cabanon Café

Lisbon, Portugal

Architect: Ternullomelo Architects
Year of completion: 2010
Gross floor area: 100 m²
Material: pinewood laminate flooring

Located in Parque das Nações, Lisbon, Petit Cabanon Café is a "parent and child café" – a place in which parents can relax while children play in the playroom stocked with books and toys. The space for adults remains separate – a comfortable and intimate area visually linked with the nearby playhouse through the vibrant yellows and fresh clean whites that dominate the space.

Warm lighting and materials, such as pinewood laminate flooring, enhance the homely feel, while carefully designed acoustics prevent noise from the playroom infiltrating the relaxation space. Inside the play area, the bright yellow walls, floor and ceiling pulse with energy, inviting children to play freely in a space designed to meet their every need.

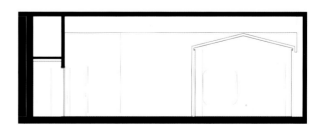

Phill Restaurant & Playground

Ilfov, Romania

Architect: Nuca Studio
Year of completion: 2011
Gross floor area: 587 m²

Located inside a multipurpose building, this vibrant café offers a meeting place designed for the entire family where architectural conventions are rejected in favor of fun. Communicating visually with the neighboring indoor playground through sculpted round openings, the café is just one of many inspiring spaces in this remarkable structure. Plastic sculpted chairs and circular tables echo the dramatically sculpted walls and ceilings, whose surfaces are perforated with transparent openings, creating sun-filled interior spaces. Inspired by vinyl toy and Manga culture, Nuca Studio sought to engage and capture the imagination of all visitors, whether children or adults: this visually intriguing and daring café interior cannot fail to do just that.

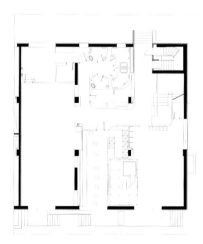
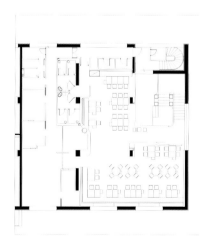

Hepb~~ 500~~
water
Iced Coffee/choc

Black Coffee	$3
Milk Coffee	$3
Soy Coffee	$4
Affogatto	$3
Hot Choc	$3·
Tea for One	$6·
Tea for Two	$4
Chai for One	$7
Chai for Two	$4
Fresh Mint Tea	$3·
Fresh Orange	$4
Fresh Blood Orange	$5
Slowpoke	
Ginger beer	$4

Slowpoke Espresso

Fitzroy, Australia

Architect: Anne-Sophie
Poirier / Sasufi
Year of completion: 2011
Gross floor area: 55m²
Material: timber

Slowpoke Espresso represents a wonderful resistance to a fast-food culture – here, both the ethos and the architecture celebrate quality food served at a slow pace. The café is located in Melbourne's oldest suburb, Fitzroy, and offers an old-fashioned, homely, warm interior. Up-cycling timber offcuts gathered from a variety of places were used to create a 12-meter-long feature wall – showcasing a range of timber species and colors, it celebrates the slow, organic growth seen in nature. Tabletops are made from recycled floorboards and other furniture and lampshades were sourced from local flea markets. This unassuming café tells the story of its own creation, of the local area, and of the vast natural world beyond, if only we have enough time to stop and look.

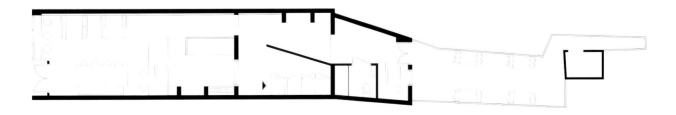

Tokyo Baby Café

Tokyo, Japan

Architect: nendo
Year of completion: 2010
Gross floor area: 205 m²

This revolutionary café allows parents to enjoy a coffee and a chat in a relaxed atmosphere, without worrying about the safety and wellbeing of their children. With aisles wide enough for prams and strollers, light switches and door handles placed out of childrens' reach, and a fabulous array of picture books and toys, the Tokyo baby café represents a haven for parent and child alike. While tables function simply as useful surfaces for adults, those same objects represent unlimited fantastical possibility for the children who play under and around them – legs become pillars and the reverse of the table top a roof covered in images of animals, a secret revealed only to the children who take advantage of this interior's exploratory potential.

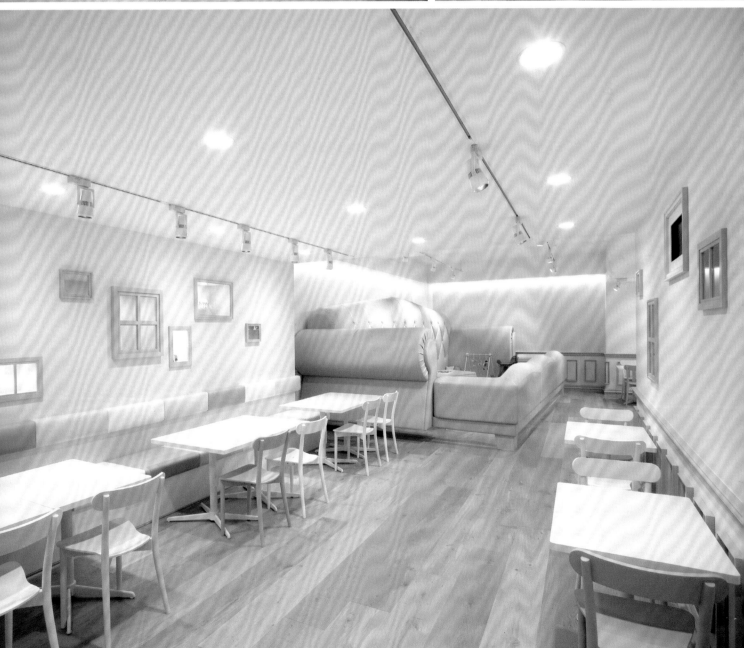

Urban Station

Buenos Aires, Argentina

Architect: Collaboration: Total Tool and Urban Station
Year of completion: 2009

Urban Station is a highly contemporary project that meets the need of today's nomadic workers. The combined office and café in Buenos Aires, Argentina, was designed by Total Tool as a space in which multiple activities – work, relaxation and socializing – can take place simultaneously, reflecting the lifestyle of the modern urban worker. The vibrant décor defies the traditional idea of an office space, yet the functionality of well-located lamps and power sockets enables any visitor to work in a relaxed, yet energetic environment. From private meeting rooms to comfy sofas, a help desk to quirky modern art, this space fully embraces the reality of modern urban life and enables visitors to live that vibrant life to the full.

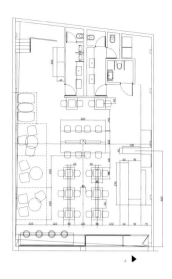

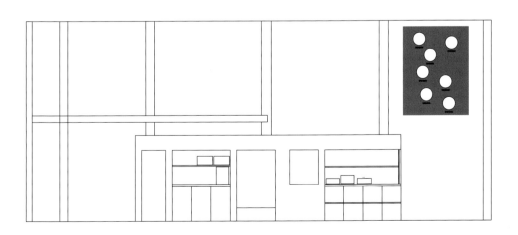

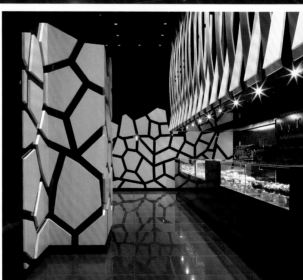

Vyta Boulangerie Italiana

Turin, Italy

Architect:
Collidanielarchitetto
Year of completion: 2011
Gross floor area: 150 m²
Material: porcelain, polymer,
oak wood, plasterboard

The food philosophy of Vyta Italian Boulangerie – nature's products enhanced by human creativity – offered the perfect inspiration for the café's architectural concept. Restraint and cool elegance were the defining principles behind the minimalist interior, which boldly declares a formal reduction to natural, essential elements. The project features contrasting materials and colors –

oak wood and corian represent tradition and innovation, while glossy black surfaces create a dramatic theatrical environment that complements the natural textures of soft oak. Lighting radiates diffusely onto the counter, enhancing the soft and intimate ambience, and hexagonal tables, reminiscent of bee-hives, pay homage to the natural world that inspired this stunning café interior.

La Natura offre elementi
semplici: acqua, grano e fuoco.
La mano esperta, la pazienza
e la creatività dell'uomo creano
da millenni forme, sapori
e profumi fragranti:
il pane alimentazione
dell'umanità antica e moder

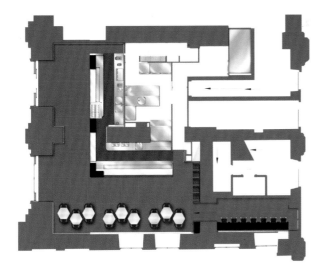

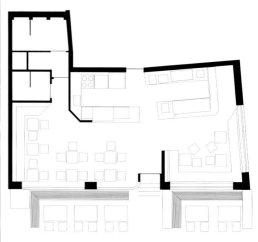

186

Z am Park

Zurich, Switzerland

Architect: Aekae: Fabrice
Aeberhard / Christian Kaegi
Year of completion: 2009
Gross floor area: 75 m²
Material: concrete, oak, brass

This understated interior was designed by Aekae for a café in a Zurich park – in this space, the natural world can be contemplated and enjoyed without any flashy architectural distractions. Beautiful oak parquet flooring from the building has been re-appropriated in the bar and benches, while old curtains were used to fashion the upholstery and a modular vintage lamp provides cozy illumination. The chairs, customized by various artists and designers, are replaced every three months with new designs – a quirky feature in this unusual café. This is a beautiful interior that refuses to draw attention to itself, instead providing the perfect setting in which to escape the bustle of urban life and dwell in peaceful coexistence with the natural world.

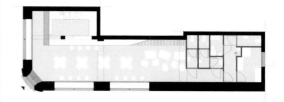

zmianatematu

Lodz, Poland

Architect: xm3
Year of completion: 2011
Gross floor area: 104 m²
Material: plywood

With a very small budget, xm3 have created a sublime space that's perfect for hosting cutting-edge artistic and cultural events. The radical, highly contemporary design reflects the aspirations and vibrant youth culture of the city of Lodz. Timber stalactites curve downwards from an undulating ceiling around the bar, generating a compelling sense of fluidity as the architecture both creates and enters the interior space. Simple light bulbs dangle from plywood ribs, and shelves are slotted between ridges in the wall behind the bar, a visual echo of the ceiling above. Patches of plaster on the walls remind the visitor that architecture, like the cities it constructs and the people it embraces, is always a fascinating work in progress.

Index Cafés

220 Grad
>> 22

Chiemseegasse 5
5020 Salzburg (Austria)
www.220grad.com

6T7 Espai Café
>> 18

C/Alta Maduixa, 24
17800 Olot Girona (Spain)

Aroma Espresso Bar
>> 26

161 West 72nd Street
New York, NY 10023 (USA)
www.aroma.us

Arthouse Café
>> 30

3/F Qingchun Road East
Hangzhou (China)

Bea's of Bloomsbury
>> 34

44 Theobalds Road
London WC1X 8NW
(United Kingdom)
www.beasofbloomsbury.com

Breeze Cafe
>> 36

Aria at City Center
3730 Las Vegas Boulevard
Las Vegas, NV 89158 (USA)

Café Angelikahöhe
>> 38

Hof 144
6867 Schwarzenberg (Austria)
www.angelikahoehe.at

Café Coutume
>> 42

47 Rue de Babylone
75007 Paris (France)
www.coutumecafe.com

Café del Arco
>> 46

Arco de Santo Domingo, 1
30001 Murcia (Spain)

Café Foam
>> 52

Foam Karlavägen 75
11449 Stockholm (Sweden)
www.cafefoam.com

Café Liberty
>> 58

Regent Street
London W1B 5AH
(United Kingdom)
www.liberty.co.uk

Café Sonja/temporary café
>> 60

Grosse Pfarrgasse 5
Vienna, 1020 (Austria)

Café Trussardi
>> 64

Piazza della Scala, 5
20121 Milan (Italy)

Cafeteria Rog
>> 66

Petkovškovo nabrežje 67
1000 Ljubljana (Slovenia)

Cielito Querido Café
>> 70

Cuauhtemoc
Mexico-City (Mexico)
www.cielitoquerido.com.mx

Dekko Cafe
>> 74

3015 Newtown Avenue
Astoria, NY 11102 (USA)
www.dekkocafe.com

D'Espresso
>> 76

317 Madison Av. on 42. St.
New York, NY 10017 (USA)
www.despresso.com

Detour Espresso Bar
>> 78

Shop 4a 135–143 William Street
Darlinghurst NSW 2010 (Australia)
www.detourcafe.com.au

Di Più
>> 80

Olympiaplatz 2
1020 Vienna (Austria)

Dishoom
>> 82

12 Upper St. Martin's Lane
London WC2H 9FB
(United Kingdom)
www.dishoom.com

El Portillo
>> 86

Javalambre Ski Station
Teruel (Spain)

Everyday Chaa
>> 90

1317, Seo-cho Dong, Seo-cho Gu
Seoul (Korea)

Federal Cafe
>> 96

C/ Parlament 39
08015 Barcelona (Spain)
www.federalcafe.es

Fonte Cafe and Wine Bar
>> 100

5412 6th Ave South
Seattle, Washington 98106 (USA)
www.fontecoffee.com

Frans Hals Museum Café
>> 104

Groot Heiligland 62
Haarlem (The Netherlands)
www.franshalsmuseum.nl

Grand Cafe Usine
>> 108

Lichttoren 6
5611 BJ Eindhoven
(The Netherlands)
www.usine.nl

Intelligentsia Coffee
>> 112

1331 Abbot Kinney Blvd.
Venice, California 90291 (USA)
www.intelligentsiacoffee.com

Ismo
>> 116

Agrinio (Greece)

Kith Café
>> 118

7 Rodyk Street, #01-33
Watermark at Robertson Quay
Singapore 238215 (Singapore)
www.kith.com.sg

Koeppe Jemp
>> 120

59, Haaptstroos
9835 Hoscheid-Dickt
(Luxembourg)

Logomo Cafe
>> 124

Köydenpunojankatu 14
20100 Turku (Finland)

Majik Café
>> 128

Džordža Vašingtona 38a
11000 Belgrade (Serbia)
www.majikcafe.com

Mazzo
>> 130

Rozengracht 114
1016 NH Amsterdam
(The Netherlands)
www.mazzoamsterdam.nl

McNally Jackson Café
>> 134

52 Prince Street
New York, NY 10012 (USA)
www.mcnallyjackson.com

Meltino Bar & Lounge
>> 140

Braga Parque -
Loja 148 (zona de fumadores) -
Quinta dos Congregados,
4710 Braga (Portugal)
www.meltino.com

Index Architects

Photo Credits